Foreclosures of Subprime Mortgages in Chicago: Analyzing the Role of Predatory Lending Practices[1]

Morgan J. Rose
Policy Analysis Division
Office of the Comptroller of the Currency

OCC Economics Working Paper 2006-1
August 2006

Abstract: A dramatic rise in subprime foreclosures over the past several years has led to calls for restrictions of, or prohibitions against, a range of lending practices loosely termed "predatory." Several cities and states have enacted legislation or regulations aimed at eliminating predatory practices, and some advocacy groups have endorsed action nationally. This working paper uses data from the Chicago metropolitan area to examine the impact of two frequently cited predatory lending practices, long prepayment penalty periods and balloon payments, on the probability of foreclosure on subprime refinance and home purchase mortgages. This paper also examines the impact of low- and no-documentation, and how combinations of low- and no-documentation, long prepayment penalty periods, and balloon payments affect foreclosure rates.

Findings indicate that the impact of each of those loan features on the probability of foreclosure varies by loan category, meaning whether the loan is a refinance or a home purchase loan, and whether the loan is a fixed-rate mortgage (FRM) or an adjustable-rate mortgage (ARM). Taken individually, long prepayment penalty periods and low- or no-documentation are associated with a greater or lesser probability of foreclosure, or have no significant association, depending on the loan category. Balloon payments are associated with greater probabilities of foreclosure for refinance FRMs, even though at the end of the sample period all of the loans in the dataset have more than two years (and most have more than five years) until their balloon payments are due. This indicates that the inability to make a balloon payment is not the direct cause of these higher foreclosure rates. Interactive effects between these loan features are also found to have sizable impacts on the probabilities of foreclosure.

These findings indicate that the relationship between predatory lending practices and foreclosure rates is more complicated than the arguments for restricting their use suggest. Policies that encourage subprime lenders to review and tighten loan underwriting and pricing procedures to ensure that borrowers' abilities to repay their loans are fully reflected in lending decisions and terms may be more effective than prohibitions on specific lending practices. This approach is consistent with the approach taken in the recently proposed Interagency Guidance on Nontraditional Mortgage Products, which emphasizes prudent loan terms and underwriting standards rather than restricting particular loan features.

[1] The views expressed in this paper are those of the author, and do not reflect those of the Office of the Comptroller of the Currency (OCC) or the Department of the Treasury. The bulk of the data collection necessary for this paper was performed by Laura St. Claire (with the OCC) and Larry Mote and Mark Hutson (both formerly with the OCC), to each of whom I am indebted.

I. Introduction

Foreclosure rates have risen strongly over the past several years, with nearly half of U.S. states seeing their numbers of foreclosures rise between 24 and 115 percent just over 2001Q4-2003Q4.[2] The dramatic increase in foreclosures has been concentrated in the subprime lending market. Many groups have cited "predatory lending practices" as a significant culprit behind the increase in subprime foreclosures, and have called for various restrictions at the local, state, and federal levels. This paper uses data for the Chicago metropolitan area, which has exhibited a large increase in foreclosures, to examine links between certain "predatory" lending practices and the probability of foreclosure on subprime refinance and home purchase mortgages.[3]

The findings indicate that the impacts of the examined loan features (described as follows) on the probability of foreclosure vary significantly across subprime refinances and home purchase mortgages, and within these categories varies further across fixed-rate mortgages (FRMs) and adjustable-rate mortgages (ARMs). In some cases, these features are even associated with reductions in the probability of foreclosure. Findings also indicate that when there is an association between a particular "predatory" loan feature and a greater probability of foreclosure, the feature may not drive the association; rather, some associations appear driven by characteristics of the lender, the borrower, or both, that are not fully captured in the available data.

These results weaken the case for federal legislation, such as the enactment of a national predatory lending law, or regulatory action to restrict these "predatory" lending practices. The effect of predatory lending practices on foreclosure rates appears more complex than a superficial view would suggest, raising the probability of unexpected and undesired consequences arising from broad restrictions or prohibitions of these practices. A sounder approach may be for lenders, regulators, and other major players (such as government-sponsored enterprises) to emphasize prudent loan terms and underwriting standards rather than restricting specific loan features.

The remainder of this paper is structured as follows. Section II provides background information on predatory lending practices and previous literature on the subject. Section III describes this paper's data sources and the econometric methodology for examining the data. Section IV presents results from the empirical analysis, and implications derived from the results are discussed in Section V. Section VI concludes.

---

[2] Federal Deposit Insurance Corporation, "Economic Conditions and Emerging Risks in Banking," April 26, 2004. (Downloaded from www.fdic.gov/deposit/insurance/risk/ecerb.pdf.)

[3] There is a substantial body of research examining Chicago subprime lending and foreclosures, most notably a series of papers from researchers affiliated with the Woodstock Institute, a Chicago nonprofit organization that advocates greater governmental restrictions on subprime lending. These studies document that the number of foreclosure starts in Chicago rose from 4,046 in 1995 to 18,213 in 2002 (Immergluck and Smith, 2005).

II. Background

<u>What Is Predatory Lending?</u>

The phrase "predatory lending" has no precise or agreed-upon meaning, but generally refers to loan terms or lending practices that result in more onerous terms for a borrower than is warranted given a borrower's background and financing needs. Engel and McCoy (2002) defined predatory lending as "a syndrome of abusive loan terms or practices that involve one or more of the following problems:

(1)   loans structured to result in seriously disproportionate net harm to borrowers;
(2)   harmful rent seeking;
(3)   loans involving fraud or deceptive practices;
(4)   other forms of lack of transparency in loans that are not actionable as fraud; and
(5)   loans that require borrowers to waive meaningful legal redress."

They acknowledge that this definition is not suitable as a statutory definition for predatory lending, instead offering it as "a diagnostic tool for identifying problematic loan terms that require redress."[4]

In empirical research and in legislation and regulations that have been proposed and enacted, predatory lending is generally defined using a list of particular loan terms or lending practices. Predatory lending defined in this manner is often taken to encompass one or more of the following:[5]

(1)   Interest rates significantly higher (the number of percentage points varies but usually falls within 5 to 8 percent) than Treasury securities of comparable maturities.
(2)   Long prepayment penalty periods, especially those lasting three years or more.
(3)   Balloon payments.
(4)   Excessively high points or fees.
(5)   Lending based on borrowers' asset values rather abilities to repay.
(6)   Frequent refinancing ("flipping") without financial benefit for borrowers.
(7)   Steering customers who qualify for lower-cost credit into higher-cost loans.
(8)   Insufficient disclosure of the costs or risks associated with a loan.
(9)   Inflated appraisals or income figures.

In its guidelines and advisory letters, the OCC similarly has described predatory lending using lists of practices rather than a single definition.[6] While OCC communications have stated "a fundamental characteristic of predatory lending is the aggressive marketing of credit to prospective borrowers who simply cannot afford the credit on the terms being offered," they also

---

[4] Engel and McCoy (2002), pages 1260-1261.
[5] A more exhaustive list of lending practices considered predatory can be found in Sturdevant and Brennan (1999), and is reproduced in Engel and McCoy (2002), footnote 6.
[6] For examples, see "OCC Guidelines Establishing Standards for Residential Mortgage Lending Practices" (2005), OCC Advisory Letter 2003-2 ("Guidelines for National Banks to Guard Against Predatory and Abusive Lending Practices"), OCC Advisory Letter 2003-3 ("Avoiding Predatory and Abusive Lending Practices in Brokered and Purchased Loans"), and OCC Advisory Letter 2000-7 ("Abusive Lending Practices").

note "it is generally necessary to consider the totality of the circumstances to assess whether a loan is predatory."[7]

Previous Literature

Two studies by Immergluck and Smith (2004 and 2005), in affiliation with the Woodstock Institute, make a case for stricter regulation of subprime lending using Chicago-area data. Immergluck and Smith (2004) present evidence that subprime (purchase and refinance) mortgages are far more strongly associated with foreclosures than prime mortgages. In Immergluck and Smith (2005), they show that each foreclosure results in significant reductions in value of nearby single-family homes, with their calculations indicating that each Chicago foreclosure results in average cumulative property value losses of $159,000-$371,000 per foreclosure for the surrounding homes, depending on the assumptions used.

Combining the results of these papers creates the argument that:

(1) The expansion of subprime (compared to prime) mortgages is associated with a large increase in foreclosures.
(2) Foreclosures are associated with significant negative externalities in the form of lost wealth and decreased tax bases.
(3) Social welfare may be enhanced by restricting subprime lending, even if this also prevents some subprime borrowers from receiving beneficial credit.[8]

However, little previous analysis has been conducted on the effects of predatory lending practices on subprime foreclosures. Most of the literature on predatory lending has examined the impact of specific anti-predatory lending laws on the quantity of subprime loans originated and the prevalence of the loan features and lending practices the laws target.

Harvey and Nigro (2003) found that after Chicago passed one of the earliest municipal predatory lending laws, which imposed sanctions on banks that make loans with interest rates five percentage points higher than Treasury securities with comparable maturities, banks moved away from subprime lending, but nonbank lenders (not covered by the law) largely filled the gap, resulting in a relatively small reduction in subprime originations. A more extensive state anti-predatory law passed in 1999 in North Carolina prohibited prepayment penalties on low-value mortgages, and prohibited balloon payments, negative amortization products, and lending without regard to borrower's ability to repay in loans with fees in excess of 5 percent or interest rates more than 8 percentage points above comparable Treasury securities. An analysis by Quercia, Stegman, and Davis (2003) showed that this law did curtail the frequency of long prepayment penalty periods and balloon payments in subprime refinance loans. Harvey and Nigro (2004) also examined the North Carolina law and found that overall subprime lending

---

[7] OCC Advisory Letter 2003-2 ("Guidelines for National Banks to Guard Against Predatory and Abusive Lending Practices"), page 2.

[8] This argument in favor of placing greater restrictions on subprime lending does not address the soundness and safety of the banking or mortgage lending industries. The focus is instead on the effects of foreclosures on borrowers and their surrounding communities. For that reason, the analysis of the present paper also ignores the potential effects of predatory lending restrictions on banks and other mortgage lenders, and is confined to examining whether the predatory lending practices in question are associated with higher or lower probabilities of foreclosure.

4

contracted subsequent to passage, driven mainly by a fall in application volume, and affecting nonbank subprime lending more, and more quickly, than bank subprime lending.

Li and Ernst (2006) examined differences in the prevalence of subprime loans with predatory features, the volume of subprime originations, and initial interest rates on subprime loans between states that had anti-predatory lending laws and states that did not. Using data covering 1998-2004, they found that states with anti-predatory laws had a lower percentage of subprime loans with predatory features (which they defined as prepayment penalties of any duration, balloon payments, and borrowers with high credit scores and full documentation), no difference in overall subprime mortgage volume, and similar or lower subprime interest rates, compared to states without such laws. Ho and Pennington-Cross (2006) create an index of anti-predatory laws to analyze their impact on subprime applications, originations, and rejection rates. Their results indicate that the typical anti-predatory law has little impact on applications and originations, but does reduce rejections. Their study also shows that laws with more extensive restrictions or prohibitions can have significant impacts on applications and originations as well as rejections.

Although these studies do address predatory lending practices, variously defined, they do not examine the impacts of predatory lending practices specifically on foreclosures. One of the only studies to do so is the Quercia, Stegman, and Davis (2005) study (hereafter QSD). Using nationwide data on subprime refinance loans originated in 1999 and tracked through 2003, they find that long prepayment penalty periods and balloon payments are associated with a significant increase in the probability of foreclosure.[9]

The present paper performs an analysis similar to that of QSD, but with substantive differences. While QSD examine only refinance loans and pool FRMs and ARMs together, this paper addresses loans that are divided by loan purpose (refinance or purchase) and loan type (FRM or ARM) into four loan categories, so that differences among loan categories can be identified. Also, the interactive effects of the examined loan features are explicitly investigated here, allowing for somewhat deeper analysis of the impacts of certain lending practices on the probability of foreclosure. Additionally, although QSD use low- or no-documentation as a control variable, greater attention is paid to this variable here to examine how less demanding information requirements for borrowers can affect foreclosure rates across loan categories, and in particular the effects of the interactions of low- or no-documentation with long prepayment penalty periods and balloon payments.

This paper uses data from Chicago originations from the start of 1999 through mid-2003, rather than focusing on a single cohort (1999 originations) from across the country as in QSD. Narrowing the geographic range of the investigation limits regional forces that could potentially cloud the results, but restricts the number of loans available for study. This negative effect is mitigated by the extension of the temporal range of originations included. QSD's analysis incorporates variables to control for state-level effects that are not relevant here, while this paper

---

[9] QSD's findings also indicate that a loan being an ARM rather than a FRM is associated with a greater increase in the probability of foreclosure than either a long prepayment penalty period or a balloon payment, an unexpected result that is also found in this paper's data in unreported results.

incorporates several demographic control variables at the ZIP code area level not present in QSD.

III. Data and Methodology

In this section, the data, their sources, and the methodology employed in this paper's analysis are described. I also present motivating evidence for analyzing for each of the four loan categories separately (refinance FRM, refinance ARM, purchase FRM, and purchase ARM) the relationships between foreclosure rates and long prepayment penalty periods, balloon payments, and low- or no-documentation. In Section IV, results are provided from econometric estimation of the impact of these loan features on the probability of foreclosure, controlling for the impacts of a variety of other loan and demographic characteristics (detailed as follows).

A multinomial logit model was selected for the econometric analysis. This model estimates the impact explanatory variables have on the probability of one outcome (such as a foreclosure) relative to other outcomes (such as a loan remaining active or being prepaid). A brief description of the multinomial logit model, and the rationale for its selection, is provided in Appendix A. To include time-varying covariates, the data was converted into "event history" format, meaning that each quarter that a loan is active represents one observation. Each observation (loan-quarter) includes a variable indicating whether by the end of the quarter the loan remained active, saw its first foreclosure start, or was prepaid.[10] If a loan has been prepaid or seen its first foreclosure start in a given period, it is no longer in the sample in subsequent periods. The multinomial logit model requires that the probabilities of the possible outcomes sum to one, enabling the straightforward handling of the competing risks of foreclosure and prepayment. To control for unobserved heterogeneity and possible dependence among loan-quarter observations for the same loan, all econometric estimation was performed using robust standard errors allowing for clustering by loan.[11]

The dataset used in this paper was purchased from LoanPerformance, Inc., a supplier of mortgage finance, servicing, and securitization information, and analytical products. The dataset consists of quarterly loan-level data on subprime refinance and home purchase mortgages on properties in the Chicago metropolitan area (specifically, ZIP codes beginning with 606) that have been packaged into private-label mortgage-backed securities. Although the data includes loans originated from 1971 through the second quarter of 2003, it has relatively few loans per year until the late 1990s.[12] Therefore, the analysis here uses only loans originating on or after

---

[10] Because of the discretion lenders have in whether and when to begin foreclosure proceedings, a measure of delinquency or default might be better suited as an outcome to portray borrower distress. However, the arguments in favor of restrictions against predatory lending practices tend to stress the negative externalities of foreclosure to justify regulatory action. That, and the availability of first foreclosure start dates in the LoanPerformance data, motivates the use of first foreclosure start here.

[11] Preferably, the econometric analysis also would incorporate lender fixed effects, or at least control for the type of lender (bank, broker, etc.). The dataset used for this paper, described as follows, does not identify originating lenders and has too many missing values for lender type (86 percent of the sample) to use that variable. Other potentially useful information about the supply side of the market, such as concentration of lenders by ZIP code area, also is not readily available.

[12] The number of loans included in the LoanPerformance dataset for Chicago doubled or tripled each year between 1995 (149 loans) and 1998 (4,325 loans), nearly doubled between 1998 and 1999 (7,441 loans), then grew at a more measured pace through 2002 (10,360 loans), the last full year in the dataset. Quercia, Stegman, and Davis (2003)

January 1, 1999, after which the LoanPerformance data more plausibly encompasses a substantial portion of the Chicago subprime market (and after which the number of missing values for several variables is markedly lower).

This relatively short time period causes two notable limitations. First, the mortgages included in the sample are relatively unseasoned, so the following empirical results may not reflect long-term mortgage performance. Second, because the sample period ends in mid-2003, some non-traditional mortgage types that have become widespread more recently, such as payment-option loans, are not represented. The following results, therefore, may not apply to such potentially important loan types.

The LoanPerformance data contains loan-level information, including purpose (refinance or purchase), type (FRM or ARM), origination date, date of first foreclosure start (if any), loan-to-value ratio at origination, borrower FICO score at origination, whether the borrower withdrew cash out (for refinances), whether the loan terms were based on low- or no-documentation, the length of prepayment penalty period (if any), and whether the loan required a balloon payment.[13]

LoanPerformance does not include borrower demographic characteristics, so data from the 2000 Census served as proxies.[14] Specifically, the median household income, the percentage of residents who are black, the percentage who are Hispanic, the percentage who have at least a high school diploma or its equivalent, and the average number of adults per household were collected for each locale (defined by ZIP code) in the sample. Also included are interest rate indices taken from the Federal Housing Finance Board.[15] The exclusion of observations with missing values resulted in the final dataset comprising more than 200,000 loan-quarter observations tracking 32,618 loans.[16] Definitions and sources for all of the variables used in the empirical analysis are provided in Table 1, and summary statistics are provided by loan category in Table 2. Table 3 presents t-statistics indicating significant differences (at the 0.1 percent level in most cases) in means for most variables across all four loan categories, supporting the splitting of the sample by loan category.

---

estimate that by 1999 LoanPerformance data covered more than 40 percent of the nationwide subprime market, but do not provide state- or city-level estimates.

[13] The LoanPerformance data includes the initial and current interest rates for each loan, but 42 percent of the sample observations have a value of zero, which I take to indicate a missing value, in one or both of these fields. As such, I do not include these variables in the following analysis.

[14] An attempt was made to combine the LoanPerformance data with publicly available data reported under Home Mortgage Disclosure Act of 1975 (HMDA), which includes borrower demographic information. However, there is not enough overlap of information to match reliably observations across datasets for each loan. A large majority could be matched by linking ZIP codes (included in LoanPerformance data) to census tracts (included in HMDA data), but the variability of ZIP codes over time, the fact that census tracts often straddle ZIP codes, and the sheer number of census tracts in the Chicago area combine to make this a prohibitively time consuming process.

[15] Most foreclosure studies also include a housing price index to control for trends in house values. An index for the Chicago MSA from the Federal Home Loan Mortgage Corporation was initially included here, but it rose so steadily over the sample period that its correlation with loan age was greater than 90 percent, requiring it to be dropped.

[16] Only 27 refinance ARMs (255 observations) and 8 purchase ARMs (98 observations) feature a balloon payment. Including the *BALLOON* indicator variable in models using only ARM loans prevented convergence of the parameter estimates, so these 35 loans were removed from the sample and *BALLOON* was dropped from ARM-only models. Sixty-three interest-only ARMs (196 observations) were also removed from the sample, although the results shown below are not substantially altered if these loans are included.

Table 1: Variable Definitions and Sources

Variable	Definition	Source
Loan Features:		
PREPAY36	Equals 1 if the loan has a prepayment penalty period longer than 36 months from origination; equals 0 otherwise	LoanPerformance
BALLOON	Equals 1 if the loan has a balloon payment; equals 0 otherwise	LoanPerformance
LOWNODOC	Equals 1 if the loan is a low- or no-documentation loan; equals 0 otherwise	LoanPerformance
Loan Characteristic Controls:		
FICO	Borrower's FICO score at origination	LoanPerformance
AGEOFLOAN	Age of the loan (months since origination)	LoanPerformance
LTV	Loan-to-value ratio at origination	LoanPerformance
CASHOUT	Equals 1 if the loan is a cashout refinancing; equals zero otherwise	LoanPerformance
Macroeconomic and Demographic Controls:		
$\Delta INTRATE$	Change in the average effective interest rate since origination[17]	FHFB's Monthly Interest Rate Survey
INCOME	Median household income for the borrower's locale (defined by ZIP code), in thousands	2000 Census
%BLACK	Percent of population in the borrower's locale (defined by ZIP code) that is black	2000 Census
%HISPANIC	Percent of population in the borrower's locale (defined by ZIP code) that is Hispanic	2000 Census
ADULTS/HH	Average number of adults (eighteen years old or older) per household in the borrower's locale (defined by ZIP code)	2000 Census
%HIGHSCHOOL	Percent of population in the borrower's locale (defined by ZIP code) that has at least a high school diploma or equivalent	2000 Census
Vintage Controls:		
1999	Equals 1 if the loan originated in 1999; equals 0 otherwise	LoanPerformance
2000	Equals 1 if the loan originated in 2000; equals 0 otherwise	LoanPerformance
2001	Equals 1 if the loan originated in 2001; equals 0 otherwise	LoanPerformance
2002/03	Equals 1 if the loan originated in 2002 or the first two quarters of 2003; equals 0 otherwise	LoanPerformance

[17] The effective interest rate is the interest rate reflecting amortization of initial fees and charges. The Federal Housing Finance Board (FHFB) provides monthly estimates of national average effective interest rates.

Table 2: Summary Statistics

	Refinance FRMs					Refinance ARMs				
	Obs.	Mean	St. Dev.	Min.	Max.	Obs.	Mean	St. Dev.	Min.	Max.
PREPAY36	69,754	0.142	0.349	0	1	105,740	0.087	0.281	0	1
BALLOON	76,036	0.386	0.487	0	1	109,208	0	0	0	0
LOWNODOC	64,699	0.156	0.363	0	1	108,453	0.222	0.416	0	1
FICO	76,036	612.189	63.843	400	850	109,208	585.942	57.743	350	850
AGEOFLOAN	76,031	17.141	12.462	1	54	109,198	13.348	10.358	1	54
LTV	76,036	76.336	17.712	11	125	109,208	76.474	11.942	10	121.38
CASHOUT	76,036	0.873	0.333	0	1	109,208	0.826	0.379	0	1
ΔINTRATE	76,031	-0.357	0.845	-2.950	1.610	109,198	-0.395	0.683	-2.880	1.610
INCOME	75,624	35.455	9.484	14.205	100.377	108,774	36.277	9.517	14.205	100.377
%BLACK	75,624	62.804	35.944	0.363	98.198	108,774	54.375	37.599	0.363	98.198
%HISPANIC	75,624	18.829	22.383	0.695	70.367	108,774	22.817	23.735	0.695	70.367
ADULTS/HH	76,036	2.115	0.228	1.381	2.441	109,208	2.107	0.245	1.381	2.441
%HIGHSCHOOL	76,036	67.393	11.950	40.105	99.076	109,208	66.984	12.359	40.105	99.076
1999	76,036	0.478	0.499	0	1	109,208	0.281	0.450	0	1
2000	76,036	0.238	0.426	0	1	109,208	0.246	0.431	0	1
2001	76,036	0.176	0.380	0	1	109,208	0.233	0.422	0	1
2002/03	76,036	0.109	0.311	0	1	109,208	0.240	0.427	0	1

	Purchase FRMs					Purchase ARMs				
	Obs.	Mean	St. Dev.	Min.	Max.	Obs.	Mean	St. Dev.	Min.	Max.
PREPAY36	16,970	0.086	0.281	0	1	33,598	0.039	0.193	0	1
BALLOON	17,672	0.477	0.499	0	1	34,224	0	0	0	0
LOWNODOC	16,718	0.290	0.454	0	1	34,091	0.246	0.431	0	1
FICO	17,672	637.916	62.067	438	850	34,224	617.166	62.766	427	850
AGEOFLOAN	17,671	13.434	10.561	1	54	34,219	12.399	9.806	1	54
LTV	17,672	88.262	10.938	19.16	125.00	34,224	83.417	8.398	26.00	100.00
CASHOUT	17,672	0	0	0	0	34,224	0	0	0	0
ΔINTRATE	17,671	-0.439	0.727	-2.950	1.610	34,219	-0.402	0.649	-2.880	1.430
INCOME	17,576	36.258	10.476	14.205	100.377	34,067	36.549	10.794	14.205	100.377
%BLACK	17,576	57.215	37.193	0.363	98.198	34,067	55.296	37.580	0.363	98.198
%HISPANIC	17,576	19.595	22.121	0.695	70.367	34,067	18.981	21.710	0.695	70.367
ADULTS/HH	17,672	2.078	0.255	1.381	2.441	34,224	2.050	0.267	1.381	2.441
%HIGHSCHOOL	17,672	68.380	12.188	40.105	99.076	34,224	69.179	12.300	40.105	99.076
1999	17,672	0.253	0.435	0	1	34,224	0.213	0.410	0	1
2000	17,672	0.248	0.432	0	1	34,224	0.240	0.427	0	1
2001	17,672	0.257	0.437	0	1	34,224	0.268	0.443	0	1
2002/03	17,672	0.242	0.428	0	1	34,224	0.279	0.448	0	1

Table 2 (continued): Summary Statistics

	All Loan Categories				
	Obs.	Mean	St. Dev.	Min.	Max.
PREPAY36	226,062	0.096	0.295	0	1
BALLOON	237,140	0.159	0.366	0	1
LOWNODOC	223,961	0.212	0.408	0	1
FICO	237,140	602.737	63.078	350	850
AGEOFLOAN	237,119	14.434	11.178	1	54
LTV	237,140	78.310	14.117	10	125
CASHOUT	237,140	0.661	0.474	0	1
ΔINTRATE	237,119	-0.387	0.738	-2.950	1.610
INCOME	236,041	36.052	9.784	14.205	100.377
%BLACK	236,041	57.420	37.235	0.363	98.198
%HISPANIC	236,041	20.746	22.984	0.695	70.367
ADULTS/HH	237,140	2.099	0.245	1.381	2.441
%HIGHSCHOOL	237,140	67.536	12.232	40.105	99.076
1999	237,140	0.332	0.471	0	1
2000	237,140	0.243	0.429	0	1
2001	237,140	0.221	0.415	0	1
2002/03	237,140	0.204	0.403	0	1

Table 3: Results from t-tests for Differences of Means across Loan Categories

Numbers are t-statistics from two-tailed difference of means tests across each pair of loan categories.

	Refi FRM vs. Refi ARM	Refi FRM vs. Purch FRM	Refi FRM vs. Purch ARM	Refi ARM vs. Purch FRM	Refi ARM vs. Purch ARM	Purch FRM vs. Purch ARM
PREPAY36	36.56***	19.15***	50.68***	-0.01	29.16***	22.49***
BALLOON	---	-22.35***	---	---	---	---
LOWNODOC	-33.33***	-40.36***	-34.09***	-19.62***	-8.70***	11.14***
FICO	91.25***	-48.51***	-13.11***	-109.07***	-85.95***	34.99***
AGEOFLOAN	71.13***	36.61***	62.28***	-0.93	15.01***	11.02***
LTV	-2.14**	-85.79***	-70.91***	123.04***	-100.55***	55.79***
CASHOUT	27.52***	---	---	---	---	---
ΔINTRATE	10.61***	11.99***	8.70***	8.00***	1.65*	-6.05***
INCOME	-18.56***	-9.91***	-17.79***	0.41	-5.136***	-3.48***
%BLACK	48.29***	18.45***	32.45***	-9.34***	-3.13***	6.10***
%HISPANIC	-36.16***	-4.09***	-1.19	16.75***	26.34***	2.93***
ADULTS/HH	8.35***	19.15***	42.58***	13.96***	36.97***	12.03***
%HIGHSCHOOL	6.74***	-9.85***	-23.43***	-13.74***	-29.14***	-7.48***
1999	87.93***	55.08***	85.49***	7.98***	24.80***	9.95***
2000	-3.53***	-2.71***	-0.15	-0.72	2.53**	2.33**
2001	-29.53***	-24.93***	-34.88***	-7.27***	-12.98***	-2.27**
2002/03	-72.70***	-47.44***	-73.46***	-0.43	-14.95***	-9.40***

***Represents significance at the 1 percent level, ** the 5 percent level, * the 10 percent level.

To provide some context on how the Chicago subprime lending market compares to the market nationwide, Table 4 compares nationwide figures provided by Farris and Richardson (2004) for 2000-2002 originations (also taken from LoanPerformance data) with comparable figures for the Chicago MSA. In the Chicago sample, ARMs outnumber FRMs more than two to one, while in the nationwide sample they are approximately even.[18] The other major difference is that the Chicago sample has a much smaller proportion of loans with long prepayment penalty periods than the nationwide sample. This suggests the possibility that (for reasons not explored here) long prepayment penalty periods have a different role in the Chicago subprime lending market than they do in other locations. The extent to which this is true simultaneously implies that the following results may have limited applicability to markets outside of Chicago, and that regulation of long prepayment penalty periods nationally may have different, perhaps unanticipated, effects from one market to the next.[19] All other subprime loan characteristics are similar across the two samples.

---

[18] Farris and Richardson (2004) classify loans as FRMs, ARMs or Balloon loans, while in this paper loans are either FRMs or ARMs, with a balloon payment treated as a separate characteristic.

[19] The extent to which underwriting standards and the use of predatory lending practices vary geographically weakens the case for restricting predatory lending practices nationally. Examining cross-market variation in underwriting or predatory lending practices is beyond the scope of this paper.

Table 4: Comparison of Chicago and Nationwide Subprime Loan Characteristics, 2000-2002

	Chicago MSA		Nationwide	
	Mean	St. Dev.	Mean	St. Dev.
Refinance	0.73	0.44	0.65	0.48
Purchase	0.27	0.44	0.34	0.47
FRM	0.31	0.46	0.44	0.50
ARM	0.69	0.46	0.47	0.50
Balloon Loan	0.12	0.33	0.09	0.28
Prepayment Penalty Period > 36 Months	0.07	0.26	0.33	0.47
Full Documentation	0.75	0.43	0.73	0.45
FICO	603.46	62.90	627.94	72.33
LTV	78.76	13.55	83.56	16.11
Number of loans	24,286		1,960,283	

Nationwide data is taken from Farris and Richardson (2004). They classify loans as FRMs, ARMs, or Balloon loans, while in this paper loans are either FRMs or ARMs, with a balloon payment treated as a separate characteristic. Farris and Richardson (2004) supply a mean value for the presence of a prepayment penalty period of three years or more for 2002 originations only.

Table 5a describes the number of subprime originations for each loan category, as well as the prevalence of long prepayment penalty periods, by year of origination. Tables 5b and 5c present the same information according to the prevalence of balloon payments and low- or no-documentation, respectively. (Differing totals in originations in these and subsequent tables reflect different numbers of observations with missing values for long prepayment penalty periods, balloon payments, and low- or no-documentation.)

The number of refinance FRMs originated per year declined over the sample period, while that number increased for each of the other loan categories. For both refinance and purchase loans, there were approximately twice as many ARMs as FRMs, with the discrepancy widening for refinances and holding steady for purchases through the sample years. The prevalence of long prepayment penalty periods peaked in 2000 for most loan categories (it declined throughout the sample period for refinance ARMs). The proportion of balloon payment FRMs began dropping rapidly after 2001, more rapidly for refinance FRMs than purchase FRMs.[20] The prevalence of low- or no-documentation FRMs (refinances and purchases) rose throughout the sample period, while ARMs saw a dip in such loans in the first half of the sample period.[21]

---

[20] See footnote 16.

[21] T-test results (omitted here) indicate that for each loan category, the change in prevalence of each of the three loan features from one origination year to the next is in most cases statistically significant at the 0.1 percent level. The change in the proportion of originations with no- or low-documentation from 2002 to 2003 was not statistically significant for refinance FRMs and refinance ARMs, and was significant at the 10 percent level for purchase FRMs. The change in this proportion from 1999 to 2000 was not significant for refinance FRMs, nor was the change from 2000 to 2001 for purchase ARMs. The change in the proportion of originations with balloon payments from 2000 to 2001 was not significant, and the change in the proportion of originations with long prepayment penalty periods from 2001 to 2002 was significant at the 5 percent level. All other year-to-year changes in the proportion of originations with a given loan feature are significant at the 0.1 percent level. This might suggest against pooling loans originated in different years into one sample; however, as noted near the end of Section IV, splitting the sample by origination cohort does not alter the pattern of results reported in that section.

Table 5a: Prevalence of Long Prepayment Penalty Periods, by Loan Category and Vintage

Vintage		Refinance FRMs	Refinance ARMs	Purchase FRMs	Purchase ARMs
1999	Total originations	2,468	2,890	357	686
	Originations with $PREPAY36 = 1$	308	493	23	25
	% of total originations	**12.5%**	**17.1%**	**6.4%**	**3.6%**
2000	Total originations	1,782	2,961	482	969
	Originations with $PREPAY36 = 1$	384	353	66	71
	% of total originations	**21.5%**	**11.9%**	**13.7%**	**7 3%**
2001	Total originations	1,815	3,648	653	1,395
	Originations with $PREPAY36 = 1$	215	95	60	26
	% of total originations	**11.8%**	**2.6%**	**9.2%**	**1 9%**
2002	Total originations	1,694	5,497	925	2,043
	Originations with $PREPAY36 = 1$	167	117	57	59
	% of total originations	**9.9%**	**2.1%**	**6.2%**	**2 9%**
2003 (first two quarters only)	Total originations	637	1,616	286	644
	Originations with $PREPAY36 = 1$	31	13	1	4
	% of total originations	**4.9%**	**0.8%**	**0.4%**	**0.6%**
1999-2003	Total originations	8,396	16,612	2,703	5,737
	Originations with $PREPAY36 = 1$	1,105	1,071	207	185
	% of total originations	**13.2%**	**6.4%**	**7.6%**	**3 2%**

Table 5b: Prevalence of Balloon Payments, by Loan Category and Vintage

Vintage		Refinance FRMs	Refinance ARMs	Purchase FRMs	Purchase ARMs
1999	Total originations	2,980	3,085	423	731
	Originations with $BALLOON = 1$	1,130	0	173	0
	% of total originations	**37.9%**	**0.0%**	**40.9%**	**0.0%**
2000	Total originations	1,868	3,093	487	981
	Originations with $BALLOON = 1$	849	0	226	0
	% of total originations	**45.5%**	**0.0%**	**46.4%**	**0.0%**
2001	Total originations	1,842	3,691	664	1,405
	Originations with $BALLOON = 1$	821	0	376	0
	% of total originations	**44.6%**	**0.0%**	**56.6%**	**0.0%**
2002	Total originations	1,713	5,539	945	2,059
	Originations with $BALLOON = 1$	317	0	421	0
	% of total originations	**18.5%**	**0.0%**	**44.6%**	**0.0%**
2003 (first two quarters only)	Total originations	637	1,617	286	644
	Originations with $BALLOON = 1$	81	0	84	0
	% of total originations	**12.7%**	**0.0%**	**29.4%**	**0.0%**
1999-2003	Total originations	9,040	17,025	2,805	5,825
	Originations with $BALLOON = 1$	3,198	0	1,280	0
	% of total originations	**35.4%**	**0.0%**	**45.6%**	**0.0%**

Recall that the small number of ARMs with balloon payments was dropped from the sample. See footnote 16.

Table 5c: Prevalence of Low- or No-Documentation, by Loan Category and Vintage

Vintage		Refinance FRMs	Refinance ARMs	Purchase FRMs	Purchase ARMs
1999	Total originations	2,090	3,040	338	727
	Originations with $LOWNODOC = 1$	312	671	42	200
	% of total originations	**14.9%**	**22.1%**	**12.4%**	**27.5%**
2000	Total originations	1,836	3,084	472	974
	Originations with $LOWNODOC = 1$	274	616	97	208
	% of total originations	**14.9%**	**20.0%**	**20.6%**	**21.4%**
2001	Total originations	1,839	3,690	658	1,405
	Originations with $LOWNODOC = 1$	335	839	173	280
	% of total originations	**18.2%**	**22.7%**	**26.3%**	**19.9%**
2002	Total originations	1,690	5,537	938	2,055
	Originations with $LOWNODOC = 1$	447	1,578	545	676
	% of total originations	**26.4%**	**28.5%**	**58.1%**	**32.9%**
2003 (first two quarters only)	Total originations	635	1,616	286	642
	Originations with $LOWNODOC = 1$	181	461	176	238
	% of total originations	**28.5%**	**28.5%**	**61.5%**	**37.0%**
1999-2003	Total originations	8,090	16,967	2,692	5,803
	Originations with $LOWNODOC = 1$	1549	4,165	1,033	1,602
	% of total originations	**19.1%**	**24.5%**	**38.4%**	**27.6%**

IV. Empirical Analysis

Tables 6 and 7 present a broad overview of the relationships between long prepayment penalty periods, balloon payments and low- or no-documentation loans and the probability of foreclosure, Table 6 shows for each loan category the percentage of loans that had a first foreclosure start in the sample period, broken out by whether a loan did or did not have the loan feature of interest. These figures indicate that for all four loan categories, loans with long prepayment penalty periods ($PREPAY36 = 1$) are more likely to have a foreclosure start than those without ($PREPAY36 = 0$). The same is true of loans with balloon payments ($BALLOON = 1$) for the two FRM loan categories, although the difference is smaller for purchase FRMs than refinance FRMs. Low- and no-documentation loans ($LOWNODOC = 1$) are less likely to have a foreclosure start in the sample period than full-documentation loans ($LOWNODOC = 0$), but the difference is much more pronounced for purchase FRMs and ARMs than for refinance FRMs and ARMs.

These figures would seem to confirm the findings of QSD, that long prepayment penalty periods and balloon payments are associated with greater probabilities of foreclosure for subprime refinance loans. Table 7, however, shows that the relationships between combinations of the loan features of interest and foreclosures are more complex. For each loan category, the top grid shows originations and foreclosures exhibiting the possible permutations of long prepayment penalty periods and balloon payments. The middle grid does the same for long prepayment penalty periods and low- or no-documentation loans, and the bottom for balloon payments and low- or no-documentation loans. The number of asterisks between two cells indicates the significance level from a t-test of their difference in foreclosure starts, as a percentage of originations. Using the top grid for refinance FRMs as an example, the difference between 8.0 percent ($PREPAY36 = 0$, $BALLOON = 0$) and 17.2 percent ($PREPAY36 = 0$, $BALLOON = 1$) is significant at the 1 percent level, while the difference between 8.0 percent and 6.6 percent ($PREPAY36 = 1$, $BALLOON = 0$) is not statistically significant.

Table 6: Originations and Foreclosure Starts by Loan Category and Loan Feature

The t-statistics are from two-tailed tests of the differences in foreclosure starts as a percentage of originations.

Panel: PREPAY36

	Refinance FRMs		Refinance ARMs		Purchase FRMs		Purchase ARMs	
	PREPAY36=0	PREPAY36=1	PREPAY36=0	PREPAY36=1	PREPAY36=0	PREPAY36=1	PREPAY36=0	PREPAY36=1
Originations	7,291	1,105	15,541	1,071	2,496	207	5,552	185
Foreclosure Starts	788	166	1,833	221	264	42	926	46
As % of Originations	10.8%	15.0%	11.8%	20.6%	10.6%	20.3%	16.7%	24.9%
	t-statistic = -4.12***		t-statistic = -8.52***		t-statistic = -4.25***		t-statistic = -2.92***	

Panel: BALLOON

	Refinance FRMs		Refinance ARMs		Purchase FRMs		Purchase ARMs	
	BALLOON=0	BALLOON=1	BALLOON=0	BALLOON=1	BALLOON=0	BALLOON=1	BALLOON=0	BALLOON=1
Originations	5,842	3,198	17,025	0	1,525	1,280	5,820	0
Foreclosure Starts	507	605	2,129	0	167	171	978	0
As % of Originations	8.7%	18.9%	12.5%	NA	11.0%	13.4%	16.8%	NA
	t-statistic = -14.33***		t-statistic = NA		t-statistic = -1.95***		t-statistic = NA	

Panel: LOWNODOC

	Refinance FRMs		Refinance ARMs		Purchase FRMs		Purchase ARMs	
	LOWNODOC=0	LOWNODOC=1	LOWNODOC=0	LOWNODOC=1	LOWNODOC=0	LOWNODOC=1	LOWNODOC=0	LOWNODOC=1
Originations	6,541	1,549	12,802	4,165	1,659	1,033	4,201	1,602
Foreclosure Starts	779	145	1,669	452	261	51	809	167
As % of Originations	11.9%	9.4%	13.0%	10.9%	15.7%	4.9%	19.3%	10.4%
	t-statistic = 2.84***		t-statistic = 3.70***		t-statistic = 8.62***		t-statistic = 8.09***	

***Represents significance at the 1 percent level, ** the 5 percent level.

15

Table 7: Originations and Foreclosure Starts by Loan Category and Loan Feature Combinations

Asterisks between two cells indicate the significance level from a two-tailed test of their difference in foreclosure starts as a percentage of originations.

	Refinance FRMs		Refinance ARMs		
	PREPAY36=0	PREPAY36=1	(category)	PREPAY36=0	PREPAY36=1
BALLOON=0			**BALLOON=0**		
Originations	5,046	411		15,551	1,071
Foreclosure Starts	403	27		1,834	221
As % of Originations	8.0% ***	6.6%		11.8% ***	20.6%
BALLOON=1			**BALLOON=1**		
Originations	2,250 *	693		0	0
Foreclosure Starts	386	139		0	0
As % of Originations	17.2%	20.1%		NA	NA
LOWNODOC=0			**LOWNODOC=0**		
Originations	5,391 ***	931		11,642 ***	886
Foreclosure Starts	604	132		1,431	187
As % of Originations	11.2% **	14.2%		12.3% ***	21.1%
LOWNODOC=1			**LOWNODOC=1**		
Originations	1,319 ***	164		3,855 ***	185
Foreclosure Starts	96	33		396	34
As % of Originations	7.3%	20.1%		10.3% ***	18.4%
LOWNODOC=0			**BALLOON=0**		
Originations	4,217 ***	2,328		12,809 ***	0
Foreclosure Starts	333	447		1,670	0
As % of Originations	7.9% ***	19.2%		13.0%	NA
LOWNODOC=1			**BALLOON=1**		
Originations	1,091 **	458		4,168	0
Foreclosure Starts	90	55		452	0
As % of Originations	8.2%	12.0%		10.8%	NA

***Represents significance at the 1 percent level, ** the 5 percent level, * the 10 percent level.

Table 7 (continued): Originations and Foreclosure Starts by Loan Category and Loan Feature Combinations

Asterisks between two cells indicate the significance level from a two-tailed test of their difference in foreclosure starts as a percentage of originations.

Purchase FRMs

		PREPAY36=0		PREPAY36=1
	BALLOON=0			
Originations		1,403	***	68
Foreclosure Starts		144		9
As % of Originations		**10.3%**		**13.2%**
			*	
	BALLOON=1			
Originations		1,094	***	139
Foreclosure Starts		120		33
As % of Originations		**11.0%**		**23.7%**
		PREPAY36=0		PREPAY36=1
	LOWNODOC=0			
Originations		1,495	***	142
Foreclosure Starts		219		35
As % of Originations		**14.6%**		**24.6%**
		***	**	
	LOWNODOC=1			
Originations		951	***	65
Foreclosure Starts		40		7
As % of Originations		**4.2%**		**10.8%**
		BALLOON=0		BALLOON=1
	LOWNODOC=0			
Originations		915	**	745
Foreclosure Starts		127		134
As % of Originations		**13.9%**		**18.0%**
		***	***	
	LOWNODOC=1			
Originations		552		481
Foreclosure Starts		31		20
As % of Originations		**5.6%**		**4.2%**

Purchase ARMs

	PREPAY36=0		PREPAY36=1
BALLOON=0			
5,557	***	185
926		46
16.7%		**24.9%**
BALLOON=1			
0		0
0		0
NA		**NA**
PREPAY36=0		PREPAY36=1
LOWNODOC=0		
4,030	**	132
772		35
19.2%		**26.5%**
***		
LOWNODOC=1		
1,513	***	52
154		11
10.2%		**21.2%**
BALLOON=0		BALLOON=1
LOWNODOC=0		
4,205		0
809		0
19.2%		**NA**
***		
LOWNODOC=1		
1,603		0
167		0
10.4%		**NA**

***Represents significance at the 1 percent level, ** the 5 percent level, * the 10 percent level.

17

Generally, the presence of a long prepayment penalty period (*PREPAY36* = 1) is associated with a greater percentage of foreclosures than the feature's absence (*PREPAY36* = 0), regardless of the presence or absence of balloon payments and low- or no-documentation loans. For refinance FRMs and purchase FRMs, however, there is no significant difference in the percentage of foreclosures for loans that do not have a balloon payment (*BALLOON* = 0). Most full-documentation loans (*LOWNODOC* = 0) are associated with a greater probability of foreclosure than low- or no-documentation loans (*LOWNODOC* = 1), but the pattern is reversed for refinance FRMs with long prepayment penalty periods. Even in loan feature combinations that have the same general pattern across loan categories, the magnitudes of the differences in foreclosure rates can vary substantially.

To establish more clearly the relationships between the loan features of interest and the probability of foreclosure, and how these relationships differ across loan categories, several multinomial logit analyses of the data were performed for each loan category.[22] Table 8 shows the results of the basic specification, in which *PREPAY36*, *BALLOON*, and *LOWNODOC* are included separately without interactions.[23] The coefficient estimates do not have an intuitive interpretation, so they are presented graphically in the charts of Figure 1. Each value in the charts represents the percentage change in the probability of a first foreclosure start, relative to the probability of a loan remaining active, associated with a one-unit change in a given explanatory variable. For example, the –19.1 percent associated with *PREPAY36* for refinance FRMs in the first page of Figure 1 indicates that the probability of a first foreclosure start (relative to that of a loan remaining active) is 19.1 percent lower for a refinance FRM with a long prepayment penalty period (*PREPAY36* = 1) than a refinance FRM without one (*PREPAY36* = 0).[24] Numbers in bold print in Figure 1 indicate estimates that are significantly different from zero at the 10 percent level or better.

---

[22] Likelihood ratio tests support splitting the full sample into the four loan categories. They also support splitting subsamples of the full sample (for example, all refinances) into the relevant loan categories (refinance FRMs and refinance ARMs). The probabilities associated with these likelihood ratio tests are all less than 0.0001.

[23] Because the focus of this paper is the impact of predatory lending practices on the probability of foreclosure, for these and subsequent specifications the results concerning the probability of prepayment are presented in Appendix B rather than alongside the results concerning the probability of a first foreclosure start.

[24] For a given coefficient estimate, β, the percentage change is calculated as $e^{\beta} - 1$. So, for example, the –0.212 shown for *PREPAY36* in the refinance FRM column coincides with $e^{(-0.212)} - 1 = -19.1$ percent in Figure 1.

Table 8: Predatory lending practices and changes in the probability of a foreclosure start

Model: Multinomial logit

Sample: Subprime loans originated on or after Jan 1, 1999; quarterly data covering 1999QI-2003QII

Note: Each coefficient estimate here represents the impact on the probability of a foreclosure start, relative to the loan remaining active, of a one-unit change in the corresponding variable. Associated results for the probability of prepayment are presented in Table B1 of Appendix B. Robust standard errors clustered by loan are in parentheses.

	Refinance FRMs	Purchase FRMs	Refinance ARMs	Purchase ARMs
PREPAY36	-0.212**	0.415**	0.016	0.082
	(.101)	(.178)	(.077)	(.174)
BALLOON	0.448***	0.007	Dropped	Dropped
	(.074)	(.122)		
LOWNODOC	0.322***	-0.362**	0.224***	-0.004
	(.106)	(.177)	(.058)	(.097)
FICO	-0.009***	-0.005***	-0.007***	-0.003***
	(.0006)	(.0011)	(.0004)	(.0006)
AGEOFLOAN	0.172***	0.149***	0.134***	0.312***
	(.018)	(.034)	(.017)	(.038)
$(AGEOFLOAN)^2$	-0.003***	-0.003***	-0.004***	-0.004***
	(.0002)	(.0004)	(.0002)	(.0004)
LTV	-0.005	-0.041***	-0.024***	0.016**
	(.004)	(.007)	(.004)	(.008)
AGEOFLOAN * LTV	0.0003*	0.0010***	0.0011***	-0.0008**
	(.0002)	(.0004)	(.0002)	(.0004)
CASHOUT	-0.155	Dropped	-0.321***	Dropped
	(.219)		(.128)	
AGEOFLOAN * CASHOUT	-0.003	Dropped	0.005	Dropped
	(.008)		(.006)	
$\Delta INTRATE$	0.175***	0.397***	0.049	0.273***
	(.070)	(.133)	(.050)	(.097)
INCOME	0.015	0.026	0.018***	-0.0008
	(.012)	(.019)	(.007)	(.010)
%BLACK	0.005**	0.015***	0.007***	0.014***
	(.003)	(.005)	(.002)	(.003)
%HISPANIC	-0.006	0.0007	-0.002	0.005
	(.005)	(.009)	(.003)	(.005)
ADULTS/HH	-0.782***	-0.638	-0.693***	-0.426
	(.313)	(.549)	(.192)	(.278)
%HIGHSCHOOL	-0.028**	-0.051***	-0.023***	-0.016
	(.012)	(.020)	(.007)	(.011)
2000	0.668***	0.910***	0.192**	0.636***
	(.129)	(.241)	(.083)	(.162)
2001	0.726***	0.728***	0.154**	1.011***
	(.131)	(.237)	(.077)	(.135)
2002/03	0.591***	1.481***	-0.256**	1.129***
	(.212)	(.298)	(.107)	(.172)
Constant	1.611	2.439	2.076***	-4.473***
	(1.140)	(1.922)	(.748)	(1.147)
# of loans:	7,774	2,639	16,505	5,700
# of foreclosure starts:	856	299	2,035	968
# of observations:	61,788	16,374	104,565	33,311
Pseudo R^2	0.079	0.103	0.090	0.093

***Represents significance at the 1 percent level, ** the 5 percent level, * the 10 percent level.

Figure 1 – Percentage Changes in the Probability of a First Foreclosure Start from a One-unit Change

<u>Note</u>: Numbers in bold are significantly different from zero at the 10 percent level

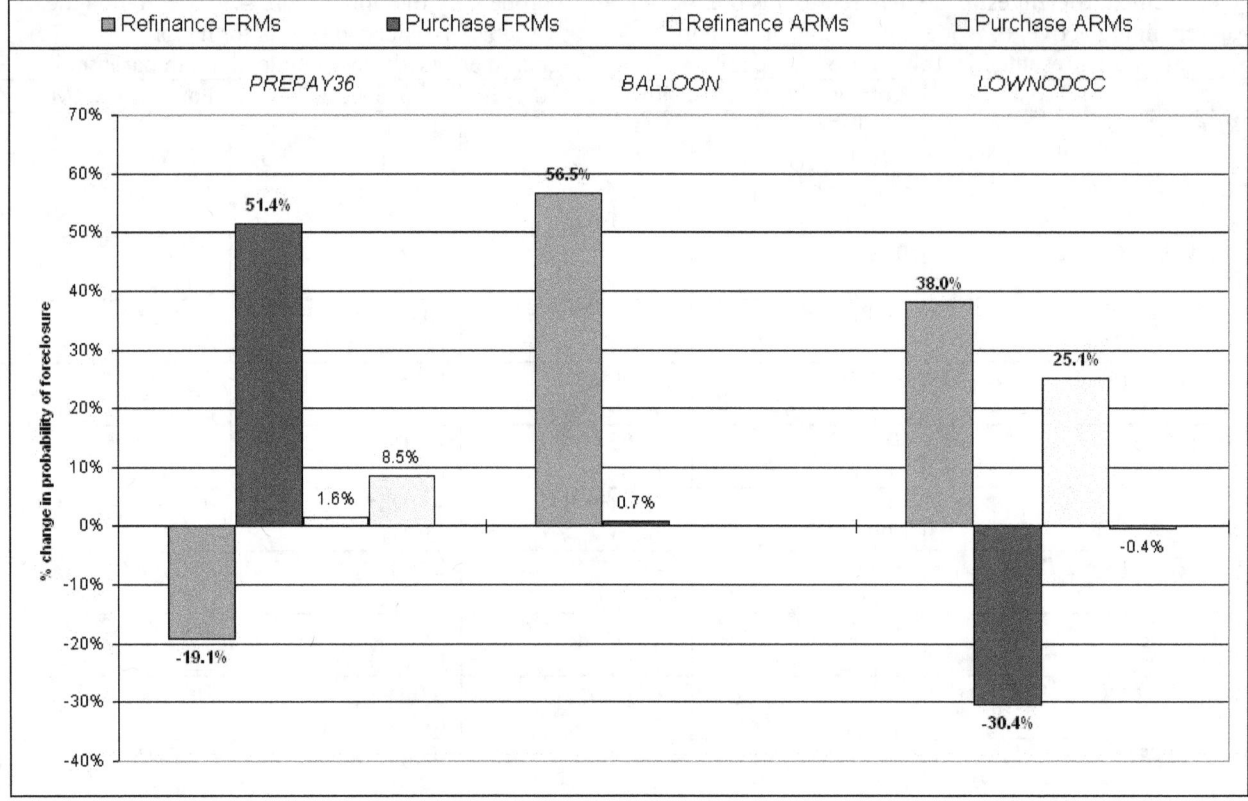

Figure 1 (continued) – Percentage Changes in the Probability of a First Foreclosure Start from a One-unit Change

Note: Numbers in bold are significantly different from zero at the 10 percent level

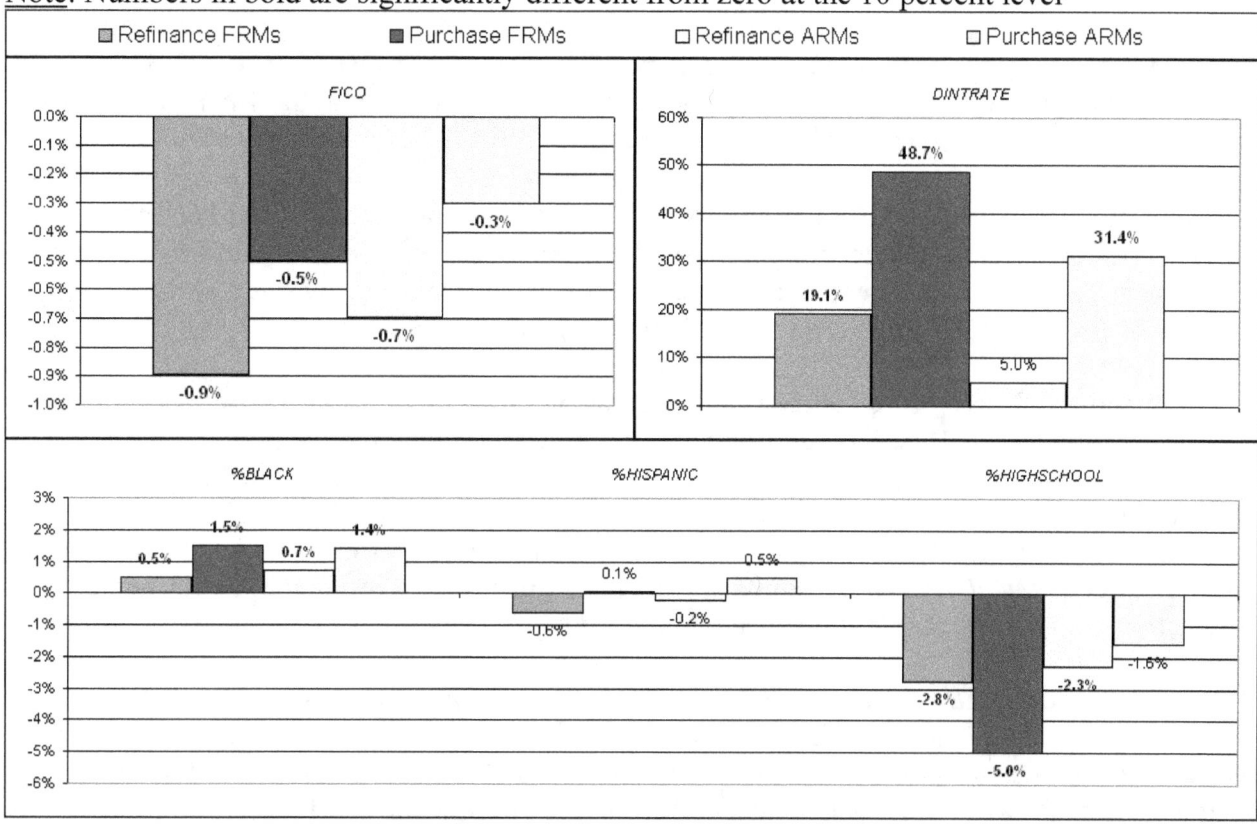

Table 8 and Figure 1 indicate that *PREPAY36, BALLOON,* and *LOWNODOC* affect the probability of foreclosure differently, depending on loan category. *PREPAY36* is associated with a lesser probability of foreclosure for refinance FRMs but a higher one for purchase FRMs, but has no statistically significant relationship with either category of ARMs. The estimates for refinance FRMs and purchase FRMs are different from each other at the 1 percent significance level, and both are different from the estimate for refinance ARMs at the 10 percent and 5 percent levels, respectively.

A refinance FRM with a balloon payment is estimated to have an almost 57 percent greater probability of foreclosure than one without a balloon payment, an impact significantly different at the 1 percent level from zero, and from the impact of *BALLOON* on a purchase FRM. (Recall that the small number of balloon ARMs was removed from the sample.)

Low- or no-documentation is associated with a greater probability of foreclosure for refinance FRMs and ARMs, a lesser probability of foreclosure for purchase FRMs, and has no significant impact for purchase ARMs. Each pair of estimates for *LOWNODOC* is significantly different at the 10 percent level or better, with the exception of the estimates for refinance FRMs and refinance ARMs.

The results for the control variables show much less variation across loan categories than those for *PREPAY36, BALLOON,* and *LOWNODOC.* With only limited exceptions, a given control

21

variable's coefficient estimates, particularly those that are significantly different from zero, tend to point in the same direction across loan categories. Charts for selected control variables are included in Figure 1.

Higher FICO scores are associated with lesser probabilities of foreclosure. The *FICO* coefficient estimates are generally significantly different from each other (usually at the 1 percent level), implying that the impact of a higher score is greater for refinance loans compared to purchase loans, and for FRMs compared to ARMs. A greater *ΔINTRATE* at origination is associated with a greater probability of foreclosure for all loan categories, except refinance ARMs. The *ΔINTRATE* coefficient estimates for purchase FRMs and purchase ARMs are different from that for refinance ARMs at the 1 percent and 5 percent levels, respectively. Figure 1 illustrates the impacts of *FICO* and *ΔINTRATE* on the probability of foreclosure.[25]

The probability of foreclosure increases at a decreasing rate with *AGEOFLOAN*. For purchase FRMs and refinance ARMs, LTV at origination is negatively related to the probability of foreclosure, while the interaction of *LTV* and *AGEOFLOAN* is positively related to it. In the short-term, a high LTV implies greater liquidity, but as a loan ages the high LTV becomes associated with a greater probability of foreclosure. For unclear reasons, this pattern is reversed for purchase ARMs. *CASHOUT* is only statistically significant for refinance ARMs, and its interaction with loan age is not significant in this study.[26]

The estimates for *ADULTS/HH* for refinance FRMs and ARMs are each significantly different from zero, indicating that one additional average number of adults per household in a locale is associated with a drop in the probability of foreclosure of 50 percent or more. Of the coefficient estimates for *INCOME*, only that for refinance ARMs is significantly different from zero.

%BLACK is associated with a greater probability of foreclosure across all loan categories. This finding is noteworthy, but unfortunately cannot be investigated more deeply with the present data. The impact of *%BLACK* is greater (at the 10 percent significance level) for purchase FRMs than for refinance FRMs, and is greater (at the 1 percent significance level) for purchase ARMs than for refinance ARMs. *%HISPANIC* is never significantly different from zero. *%HIGHSCHOOL* is associated with a lesser probability of foreclosure across all loan categories, except purchase ARMs. Figure 1 illustrates that for most loan categories, the estimated impact of an additional percent of a locale's population having at least a high school diploma or its equivalent is three or more times larger (in absolute value) than the estimated impact of an additional percent of a locale's population being black or Hispanic.

Looking at the coefficient estimates for the vintage dummies, a loan originating in any sample year other than 1999 is associated with a greater probability of foreclosure than a 1999 origination. This holds for all loan categories, except refinance ARMs.

---

[25] One unit changes, rather than one standard deviation changes, are used for the continuous variables in Figure 1 to make visual comparisons of the relative impacts of *%BLACK*, *%HISPANIC*, and *%HIGHSCHOOL* (which have substantial differences in their standard errors) more intuitive. Because the units of measurement of *FICO* and *ΔINTRATE* are different from each other and the other variables included in Figure 1, the results illustrating the effects of one-unit changes in *FICO* and *INITSPREAD* are shown in separate charts.

[26] Note that by definition a purchase loan cannot be a cashout.

As illustrated earlier in Table 7, examining the effects of combinations of long prepayment penalty periods, balloon payments, and low- or no-documentation loans can provide a more thorough understanding of those loan features' relationships with the probability of foreclosure than merely examining each feature's impact in isolation. Table 9 presents results from a specification that includes bilateral interactions of *PREPAY36*, *BALLOON*, and *LOWNODOC*, with graphical representations of the results in Figure 2. (Results for the control variables are not substantively different than those found in Table 8, and thus are omitted.)

Table 9: Interactions between predatory lending practices and changes in the probability of a foreclosure start

Model: Multinomial logit

Sample: Subprime loans originated on or after Jan 1, 1999; quarterly data covering 1999QI-2003QII

Note: The coefficient estimates here represent the impact on the probability of a foreclosure start, relative to the probability of the loan remaining active, of a one-unit change in the corresponding variable. Associated results for the probability of prepayment are presented in Table B2 of Appendix B. Robust standard errors clustered by loan are in parentheses. Results for control variables are similar to those in Table 8, and are omitted here.

	Refinance FRMs	Purchase FRMs	Refinance ARMs	Purchase ARMs
PREPAY36	-0.387**	-0.074	0.035	0.062
	(.199)	(.354)	(.084)	(.198)
BALLOON	0.506***	0.010	*Dropped*	*Dropped*
	(.085)	(.141)		
LOWNODOC	0.436***	-0.194	0.234***	-0.009
	(.137)	(.242)	(.061)	(.100)
*PREPAY36 * BALLOON*	0.109	0.699*	*Dropped*	*Dropped*
	(.228)	(.405)		
*PREPAY36 * LOWNODOC*	0.687**	0.036	-0.123	0.088
	(.283)	(.462)	(.202)	(.411)
*BALLOON * LOWNODOC*	-0.599***	-0.392	*Dropped*	*Dropped*
	(.239)	(.341)		
# of loans:	7,774	2,639	16,505	5,700
# of foreclosure starts:	856	299	2,035	968
# of observations:	61,788	16,374	104,565	33,311
Pseudo R^2	0.080	0.104	0.090	0.093

***Represents significance at the 1 percent level, ** the 5 percent level, * the 10 percent level.

Figure 2 – Percentage Changes in the Probability of a Foreclosure Start due to Loan Features and Their Interactions

<u>Note</u>: Numbers in bold are significantly different from zero at the 10 percent level

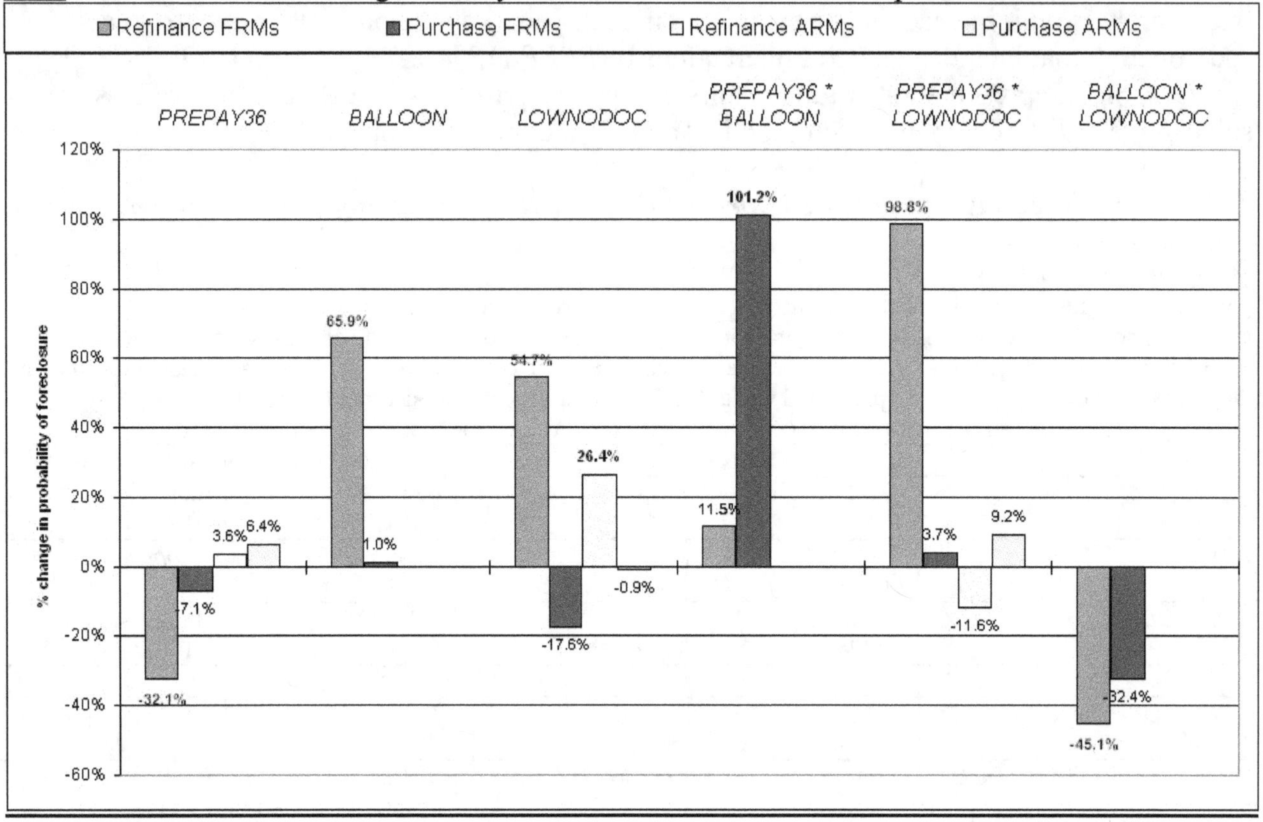

The results for the *PREPAY36*, *BALLOON,* and *LOWNODOC* (non-interacted) show a similar pattern as in the earlier specification's results; the only notable differences are that for purchase FRMs, neither *PREPAY36* nor *LOWNODOC* are statistically significant in Table 9. None of the cases, including that of purchase FRMs, have a coefficient estimate for *PREPAY36*, *BALLOON,* or *LOWNODOC* in Table 9 significantly different from its counterpart in Table 8.

The interaction term coefficient estimates show that for FRMs, but not ARMs, combinations of the loan features of interest are significantly related to the probability of foreclosure, and can have impacts of greater magnitude together than the loan features have individually.[27] For refinance FRMs, the interactive effect of a long prepayment penalty period and low- or no-documentation (separate from these features' individual effects) is almost a doubling of the probability of foreclosure. The probability increases even further if the individual effects of *PREPAY36* and *LOWNODOC* are taken into account. The total effect (not shown graphically) of both a long prepayment penalty period and low- or no-documentation, that is, of *PREPAY36*, *LOWNODOC,* and *PREPAY36*LOWNODOC* each equaling one, is positive and significant at the 5 percent level. The interactive effect (separate from the features' individual effects) of a

---

[27] Likelihood ratio tests provide strong support for including the loan feature interaction terms for refinance FRMs (probability = 0.0000), but not for purchase FRMs (0.1718), refinance ARMs (0.3743), or purchase ARMs (0.9421).

balloon payment and low- or no-documentation is associated with a drop in the probability of foreclosure of 45 percent. As a result, the total effect of having a balloon payment and low- or no-documentation is not statistically significant, despite the significance of both *BALLOON* and *LOWNODOC* individually. The total effect of having both a long prepayment penalty period and a balloon payment is positive and significant at the 10 percent level.

For purchase FRMs, the interactive effect of having both a long prepayment penalty and a balloon payment implies a doubling of the probability of foreclosure, while the effect of each of these features individually is not significantly different from zero. The total effect of having both a long prepayment penalty period and a balloon payment is positive and significant at the 1 percent level. The total effect of a balloon payment and low- or no-documentation is negative and significant at the 5 percent level, even though neither the individual nor interactive effects are themselves significant. The total effect of a long prepayment penalty period and low- or no-documentation is not significant for purchase FRMs, refinance ARMs, or purchase ARMs.

Another potential complexity in the relationships among *PREPAY36, BALLOON, LOWNODOC,* and the probability of foreclosures is the extent to which the loan features' impacts depend on borrower characteristics, such as credit history or leverage. Within each loan category, the mean *FICO* and *LTV* values for loans with and without each of the three loan features of interest were calculated. In each case, the mean value for loans with a given loan feature is within one standard deviation of the mean value for loans without that feature, suggesting that the impacts of *PREPAY36, BALLOON,* and *LOWNODOC* do not vary greatly with *FICO* or *LTV*.[28]

In August 2000, Chicago passed one of the earliest municipal anti-predatory lending statutes.[29] To ensure that the effects of this law do not drive this paper's results, an indicator variable equaling 1 if a loan originated on or after October 1, 2000, was added to the specifications previously discussed. Results were not substantively different.[30] The specifications also were run using only loans originated before October 1, 2000, then again using only loans originated on or after October 1, 2000. Each subsample contained fewer observations, resulting in higher standard errors and reductions in significance for several variables, but the same pattern of results holds in each case.

To ensure that the small number of foreclosures seen for 2003 originations does not skew the results, the specifications were run after dropping all 2003 originations. No substantive changes

---

[28] This is corroborated by two unreported regression specifications. In the first, each of the loan feature variables was interacted with indicator variables, denoting whether a given loan had a FICO score above or below the median FICO score for that loan category. The second specification was similar, using LTV values rather than FICO scores. Results from these specifications indicate that in only a few cases are there significant differences in the impact of one of the loan features depending on a high or low FICO score or LTV, with no consistent pattern either across loan categories or between the FICO score and LTV specifications.

[29] The Chicago law defined predatory lending according to the difference between the interest rate charged and that of comparable-maturity Treasury securities, rather than the presence of particular loan features. See Harvey and Nigro (2003). Their results are described on page 4.

[30] The presence of the post-law indicator variable does not affect the significance of any other variables, with the exception of the vintage indicators. In each refinance specification, the post-law indicator is significant and positive, the significances of the vintage indicators are reduced, and the sum of the coefficient estimates for the post-law indicator and *2002/03* is nearly equal to the coefficient estimate for *2002/03* shown in Table 8. In the purchase specifications, the post-law indicator is not significant, and no other coefficient estimates are appreciably affected.

to the results occurred. The results also were largely unchanged when the specifications were performed only on the 87 percent of sample loans that involved owner-occupied properties (a restriction employed by QSD). To verify that the results are not driven by the selection of the multinomial logit model, the econometric analysis discussed earlier was also run using a Cox proportional hazard model, with similar results throughout.[31]

V. Discussion of Results

The primary findings from the previous section on loan features that might be characterized as predatory are:

- Long prepayment penalty periods are not associated with greater probabilities of foreclosure for ARMs (refinances or purchases).
- Long prepayment penalty periods are associated with greater probabilities of foreclosure for purchase FRMs if the loans also feature a balloon payment.
- Long prepayment penalty periods are associated with *lesser* probabilities of foreclosure for refinance FRMs.
- Balloon payments (in the absence of long prepayment penalty periods) are only associated with greater probabilities of foreclosure for refinance FRMs.
- Low- or no-documentation is associated with greater probabilities of foreclosure for refinances, but not purchases.

These findings indicate that the relationships among long prepayment penalty periods, balloon payments, low- or no-documentation loans, and the probability of foreclosure are more complicated than many arguments for greater regulation of predatory lending practices suggest. These loan features' effects vary widely across loan categories, and their combined effects can have as important an impact on the probability of foreclosure as their individual effects.

Long prepayment penalty periods do not appear to have significant influence on the probability of foreclosure for refinance ARMs or purchase ARMs, whether or not interactive effects are considered. The positive relationship between long prepayment penalty periods and the probability of foreclosure for purchase FRMs is consistent with arguments for greater restrictions on predatory lending practices if the interactive effects of long prepayment penalty periods and balloon payments are not considered. If the interactions are considered, the combination of a long prepayment penalty period and a balloon payment doubles a loan's probability of foreclosure, but neither feature is problematic in the absence of the other.[32]

The negative relationship between long prepayment penalty periods and the probability of foreclosure for refinance FRMs is inconsistent with long prepayment penalty periods causing more foreclosures, and suggests that in some cases long prepayment penalty periods can play a useful role. One possibility is that they may act as a sorting device for borrowers' self-

---

[31] Appendix A contains a brief description of the Cox proportional hazard model. For a fuller description, see Fox (2002).

[32] Recall that for purchase FRMs, as well as both categories of ARMs, a specification with loan feature interactions is not preferred over one without interactions. For refinance FRMs, discussed next, a specification with interactions is preferred. See footnote 27.

perceptions of their ongoing ability to keep up with their mortgages. Borrowers who recognize that their future ability to make loan payments is better or more stable than their loan application and financial history portrays, may accept long prepayment penalty periods to provide a meaningful signal to lenders that they are worthwhile credit risks. Assuming that such signals may be more necessary for refinances (which a borrower may seek due to current but temporary financial difficulties) than purchases, and more credible for FRMs (with known payments throughout the loans) than ARMs, a negative relationship between long prepayment penalty periods and the probability of foreclosure for refinance FRMs would result. This explanation is consistent with the dominating increase in the probability of foreclosure associated with the presence of both a long prepayment penalty period and low- or no-documentation ($PREPAY36*LOWNODOC = 1$) – borrowers intending to send a favorable signal about their ability to repay are unlikely to actively seek reduced documentation. This is not offered as a definitive explanation for the results found, but merely as an example of how this so-called predatory lending practice could be serving a beneficial purpose for certain subprime borrowers.

Balloon payments are positively related to the probability of foreclosure for refinance FRMs but not purchase FRMs, although the interaction of long prepayment penalty periods with balloon payments has a large positive impact on the probability of foreclosure for purchase FRMs. While these findings appear to fall in line with the argument for restricting balloon payment loans, it is not evident how balloon payments are the cause of the greater probability of foreclosure. The shortest time between origination and a balloon payment coming due for this sample is seven years, with the vast majority being 10 years or more, so even a balloon loan that originated at the start of the sample period (January 1, 1999) was more than two years from having the balloon payment due at the end of the sample period (June 30, 2003). This strongly suggests that the inability of borrowers to come up with sizable balloon payments is not the cause of the greater probabilities of foreclosures on balloon loans found in this data. This, in turn, suggests that restricting the use of balloon payments would not address an underlying cause of increased foreclosures.

For both types of refinance loans, low- or no-documentation is associated with significantly greater probabilities of foreclosure. Although for refinance FRMs the effect of the interaction of balloon payments and low- or no-documentation is significant and negative, the total effect of the interaction ($BALLOON*LOWNODOC = 1$) and the features' separate impacts ($BALLOON = 1$ and $LOWNODOC = 1$) is statistically insignificant. In contrast, the only significant effect of low- or no-documentation on the probability of foreclosure for purchase loans is for purchase FRMs, and even here the effect becomes insignificant if loan feature interactions are considered (although the total effect on the probability of foreclosure of low- or no-documentation and a balloon payment is negative). These findings suggest that loosened lending standards, at least for the information required of borrowers, are significant contributors to higher probabilities of foreclosure for refinances, but not purchases.

VI. Conclusion

The results discussed earlier do not portray a subprime mortgage market in which loan features often characterized as "predatory" uniformly drive higher foreclosure rates in a consistent or straightforward manner. The reality appears much more complex, and in light of this, any proposal to address rising foreclosure rates through restricting or prohibiting particular loan features would seem unlikely to be an unmitigated success.

While long prepayment penalty periods are associated with greater probability of foreclosure for purchase FRMs, they appear to be benign in ARMs and are associated with lesser probability of foreclosure in refinance FRMs. Balloon payments are associated with greater probability of foreclosure, but this effect occurs years prior to the balloon payments coming due, calling into serious question whether the balloon payments themselves are the underlying cause. Low- and no-documentation, which may be thought of as a rough proxy for loose lending practices more generally, is unambiguously associated with greater probabilities of foreclosure for refinances and has important interactive effects when present with either long prepayment penalty periods or balloon payments. These results taken together suggest that broad regulatory action designed to restrict or prohibit the use of long prepayment penalty periods or balloon payments will likely not have the direct or sole effect of reducing subprime foreclosure rates. The use of such a blunt policy instrument would eliminate potentially valuable contractual possibilities from subprime loans, despite the fact that in many cases those loan features do not appear to be problematic.

A stronger candidate for action would be encouraging subprime lenders to review and tighten their lending practices to ensure that their borrowers, especially those seeking refinances, are not taking on more debt than they can handle given their other financial obligations, and that all information relevant to a potential borrower's ability to repay a loan is considered before extending a loan. This approach is consistent with the recently proposed Interagency Guidance on Nontraditional Mortgage Products, which encourages prudent loan terms and underwriting standards rather than restricting particular loan features. Such an approach would likely be more difficult to implement and monitor than blanket prohibitions on certain lending practices because it involves lenders' evaluation processes and relies on full disclosure by both borrower and lender. Still, this approach has the major benefits of addressing the key role that this paper's findings indicate low- or no-documentation plays, and being less likely to cause unintended and undesired distortions in the subprime lending market.

Bibliography

Cox, D.R. 1972. "Regression Models and Life-Tables." *Journal of the Royal Statistical Society, Series B (Methodological)*, Volume 34, Number 2, pages 187-220.

Engel, Kathleen C. and Patricia A. McCoy. 2002. "A Tale of Three Markets: The Law and Economics of Predatory Lending." *Texas Law Review*, Volume 80, Issue 6, pages 1255-1382.

Farris, John and Christopher A. Richardson. 2004. "The Geography of Subprime Mortgage Prepayment Penalty Patterns." Housing Policy Debate, Volume 15, Issue 3, pages 687-714.

Federal Deposit Insurance Corporation. "Economic Conditions and Emerging Risks in Banking." April 26, 2004. (Downloaded from www.fdic.gov/deposit/insurance/risk/ecerb.pdf.)

Fox, John. 2002. "Cox Proportional-Hazards Regression for Survival Data." Web appendix to John Cox, *An R and S-PLUS Companion to Applied Regression*, Thousand Oaks, CA: Sage Publications, Inc., 2002. (Downloaded from http://cran.r-project.org/doc/contrib/Fox-Companion/appendix-cox-regression.pdf.)

Greene, William H. 2000. *Econometric Analysis*, Fourth Edition (Prentice Hall, Upper Saddle River, New Jersey).

Harvey, Keith D. and Peter J. Nigro. 2004. "Do Predatory Lending Laws Influence Mortgage Lending? An Analysis of the North Carolina Predatory Lending Law." *Journal of Real Estate Finance and Economics*, Volume 29, Number 4, pages 435-456.

Harvey, Keith D. and Peter J. Nigro. 2003. "How Do Predatory Lending Laws Influence Mortgage Lending in Urban Areas? A Tale of Two Cities." *The Journal of Real Estate Research*, Volume 25, Number 4, pages 479-508.

Ho, Giang and Anthony Pennington-Cross. 2006. "The Impact of Local Predatory Lending Laws on the Flow of Subprime Credit." Working Paper 2006-009A. Federal Reserve Bank of Saint Louis.

Immergluck, Dan and Geoff Smith. 2005. "There Goes the Neighborhood: The Effect of Single-Family Mortgage Foreclosures on Property Values." Chicago, Illinois: The Woodstock Institute.

Immergluck, Dan and Geoff Smith. 2004. "Risky Business – An Econometric Analysis of the Relationship between Subprime Lending and Neighborhood Foreclosures." Chicago, Illinois: The Woodstock Institute.

Li, Wei and Keith S. Ernst. 2006. "The Best Value in the Subprime Market: State Predatory Lending Reforms." Durham, North Carolina: Center for Responsible Lending.

Office of the Comptroller of the Currency, Federal Reserve System, Federal Deposit Insurance Corporation, Office of Thrift and Supervision, and National Credit Union Administration. "Interagency Guidance on Nontraditional Mortgage Products." *Federal Register*, Volume 70, Number 249, December 29, 2005, pages 77249-77257.

Office of the Comptroller of the Currency. "OCC Guidelines Establishing Standards for Residential Mortgage Lending Practices." *Federal Register*, Volume 70, Number 24, February 7, 2005, pages 6329-6334.

Office of the Comptroller of the Currency. "OCC Advisory Letter 2003-2: Guidelines for National Banks to Guard Against Predatory and Abusive Lending Practices." February 21, 2003.

Office of the Comptroller of the Currency. "OCC Advisory Letter 2003-3: Avoiding Predatory and Abusive Lending Practices in Brokered and Purchase Loans." February 21, 2003.

Office of the Comptroller of the Currency. "OCC Advisory Letter 2000-7: Abusive Lending Practices." July 25, 2000.

Quercia, Roberto G., Michael A. Stegman and Walter R. Davis. 2005. "The Impact of Predatory Loan Terms on Subprime Foreclosures: The Special Case of Prepayment Penalties and Balloon Payments." Center for Community Capitalism, University of North Carolina at Chapel Hill.

Quercia, Roberto G., Michael A. Stegman and Walter R. Davis. 2003. "The Impact of North Carolina's Anti-Predatory Lending Law: A Descriptive Assessment." Center for Community Capitalism, University of North Carolina at Chapel Hill.

Sturdevant, Patricia and William J. Brennan, Jr. 1999. "A Catalogue of Predatory Lending Practices." *The Consumer Advocate*, Volume 5, Issue 4.

Appendix A – Multinomial Logit Model[1]

The multinomial logit model is applicable to a wide range of situations involving choice sets of multiple, unordered possible outcomes. The log-likelihood function for this model is:

$$\ln L = \sum_{i=1}^{n} \sum_{j=0}^{J} d_{ij} \ln(\text{Prob}(y_i = j))$$

with

$$\text{Prob}(y_i = j) = \frac{e^{\beta_j' X_i}}{1 + \sum_{k=1}^{J} e^{\beta_k' X_i}} \quad \text{for } j = 1, 2, \ldots, J$$

and

$$\text{Prob}(y_i = j) = \frac{1}{1 + \sum_{k=1}^{J} e^{\beta_k' X_i}} \quad \text{for } j = 0$$

where d_{ijt} is an indicator variable equaling one if outcome j occurs for loan i at time t, n_t is the number of loans active at time t, X_{it} is a vector of explanatory variable values for loan i at time t, and β_k is a vector of variable coefficients for outcome k.

The data for this paper is in event history format, meaning that each quarter that a loan is active represents one observation. For every observation, the three possible outcomes are that at the end of the quarter the loan remains active, has had a first foreclosure start, or has been prepaid. More specifically, while the original LoanPerformance data includes one observation for each loan with two date variables indicating when the first foreclosure start and prepayment (if any) occurred, the converted data includes one observation for each loan-quarter with two indicator variables showing whether a first foreclosure start or prepayment occurred for that loan in that quarter. The multinomial logit model therefore can be written more specifically for the analysis of this paper as:

$$\ln L = \sum_{t=1}^{T} \sum_{i=1}^{n_t} \sum_{j=0}^{2} d_{ijt} \ln(\text{Prob}(y_{it} = j))$$

with

$$\text{Prob}(y_{it} = j) = \frac{e^{\beta_j' X_{it}}}{1 + \sum_{k=1}^{J} e^{\beta_k' X_{it}}} \quad \text{for } j = 1, 2$$

and

---

[1] This description of the multinomial logit model draws largely from Greene (2000).

31

$$\text{Prob}(y_{it} = j) = \frac{1}{1 + \sum\limits_{k=1}^{J} e^{\beta k' Xit}} \quad \text{for } j = 0$$

where d_{ijt} is an indicator variable equaling one if outcome j occurs for loan i at time t, X_{it} is a vector of explanatory variable values for loan i at time t, and β_k is a vector of variable coefficients for outcome k. The j values 0, 1, and 2 refer to a loan remaining active, having a first foreclosure start, and being prepaid, respectively. Because the model requires that the sum of the probabilities of all possible outcomes equal one, this model directly controls for the competing risks of foreclosure and prepayment.

The multinomial model assumes that the odds ratio between any two outcomes is independent of any alternative outcomes (the "independence of irrelevant alternatives" assumption). An alternative model that could be used is the Cox proportional hazard model, a widely used model for survival data that allows for the estimation of the effect of explanatory variables on survival times without requiring any assumptions about the nature or shape of the underlying hazard function. This model requires the assumption that given two observations with different values for the independent variables, the ratio of the observations' hazard functions does not depend on time (the "proportionality assumption"). Because it is not clear which assumption, and therefore which model, better fits the reality of the subprime mortgage market, the selection of one model over the other was not straightforward. The multinomial logit model was ultimately selected because it allows easier hypothesis testing across specifications. While the Cox model does not need an assumed specification for the underlying hazard, which is generally an advantage, it makes hypothesis testing across specifications problematic. Given that a major emphasis of this paper is that the relationship between the loan features of interest and the probability of foreclosure varies across loan categories, the ability to assign statistical significance levels to coefficient estimate differences across loan categories was the decisive factor in favor of the multinomial logit model. As a robustness check, all of the econometric analyses performed in this paper using the multinomial logit model were also performed using the Cox proportional hazard model. The two sets of results were similar in the magnitudes and statistical significances of the coefficient estimates in all specifications.

Appendix B – Multinomial Logit Results for the Probability of Prepayment

The tables in this appendix provide the multinomial logit results for the probability of prepayment (relative to the probability of a loan remaining active) that coincide with the results for the probability of foreclosure presented in Tables 8 and 9. Although the main focus of the paper is the relationship between the loan features of interest and the probability of foreclosure, these results for the probability of prepayment are presented in the interest of completeness.

Table B1: Predatory lending practices and changes in the probability of prepayment
Model: Multinomial logit
Sample: Subprime loans originated on or after Jan 1, 1999; quarterly data covering 1999QI-2003QII
Note: The coefficient estimates here represent the impact on the probability of prepayment, relative to the loan remaining active, of a one-unit change in the corresponding variable. Associated results for the probability of a foreclosure start are presented in Table 8. Robust standard errors clustered by loan are in parentheses.

	Refinance FRMs	Purchase FRMs	Refinance ARMs	Purchase ARMs
PREPAY36	-0.170***	-0.056	-0.014	-0.229*
	(.063)	(.136)	(.054)	(.137)
BALLOON	-0.069	-0.384***	Dropped	Dropped
	(.045)	(.076)		
LOWNODOC	0.305***	0.082	0.143***	0.182***
	(.055)	(.089)	(.035)	(.065)
FICO	-0.002***	0.002***	0.0001	0.0004
	(.0003)	(.0006)	(.0002)	(.0004)
AGEOFLOAN	0.177***	0.194***	0.201***	0.158***
	(.011)	(.035)	(.010)	(.028)
$(AGEOFLOAN)^2$	-0.003***	-0.004***	-0.004***	-0.004***
	(.0002)	(.0004)	(.0001)	(.0003)
LTV	-0.011***	-0.011*	-0.018***	-0.030***
	(.002)	(.007)	(.002)	(.007)
AGEOFLOAN * LTV	0.0001	0.0005	0.0006***	0.0011***
	(.0001)	(.0004)	(.0001)	(.0003)
CASHOUT	-0.054	Dropped	0.084	Dropped
	(.124)		(.085)	
AGEOFLOAN * CASHOUT	-0.005	Dropped	-0.007*	Dropped
	(.005)		(.004)	
ΔINTRATE	-0.041	0.078	-0.013	-0.044
	(.045)	(.095)	(.034)	(.068)
INCOME	-0.008	-0.0003	-0.009**	-0.004
	(.006)	(.009)	(.004)	(.006)
%BLACK	-0.008***	-0.011***	-0.009***	-0.008***
	(.0013)	(.002)	(.0009)	(.001)
%HISPANIC	-0.0005	-0.011**	-0.0005	0.001
	(.003)	(.005)	(.002)	(.003)
ADULTS/HH	-0.234	-0.497**	-0.219**	-0.285
	(.171)	(.248)	(.110)	(.170)
%HIGHSCHOOL	0.001	-0.020**	0.005	0.0007
	(.007)	(.011)	(.004)	(.007)
2000	0.315***	0.627***	0.064	0.146
	(.080)	(.175)	(.056)	(.109)
2001	0.921***	1.232***	0.360***	0.528***
	(.075)	(.164)	(.050)	(.096)
2002/03	0.976***	1.244***	0.460***	0.555***
	(.102)	(.206)	(.064)	(.123)
Constant	-2.211***	-2.852**	-3.346***	-2.367***
	(.662)	(1.219)	(.464)	(.876)
# of loans:	7,774	2,639	16,505	5,700
# of prepayments:	2,574	859	5,521	1,696
# of observations:	61,788	16,374	104,565	33,311
Pseudo R^2	0.079	0.103	0.090	0.093

***Represents significance at the 1 percent level, ** the 5 percent level, * the 10 percent level.

Table B2: Interactions between predatory lending practices and changes in the probability of prepayment

Model: Multinomial logit
Sample: Subprime loans originated on or after Jan 1, 1999; quarterly data covering 1999QI-2003QII
Note: The coefficient estimates here represent the impact on the probability of prepayment, relative to the probability of the loan remaining active, of a one-unit change in the corresponding variable. Associated results for the probability of a foreclosure start are presented in Table 9. Robust standard errors clustered by loan are in parentheses. Results for control variables are similar to those in Table B1, and are omitted here.

	Refinance FRMs	Purchase FRMs	Refinance ARMs	Purchase ARMs
PREPAY36	-0.371***	-0.178	0.016	-0.206
	(.110)	(.245)	(.059)	(.167)
BALLOON	-0.069	-0.303***	Dropped	Dropped
	(.053)	(.093)		
LOWNODOC	0.427***	0.212*	0.155***	0.184***
	(.067)	(.115)	(.036)	(.066)
PREPAY36 * BALLOON	0.400***	0.198	Dropped	Dropped
	(.131)	(.280)		
PREPAY36 * LOWNODOC	-0.289*	0.028	-0.164	-0.075
	(.178)	(.280)	(.131)	(.289)
BALLOON * LOWNODOC	-0.298***	-0.332**	Dropped	Dropped
	(.118)	(.164)		
# of loans:	7,774	2,639	16,505	5,700
# of prepayments:	2,574	859	5,521	1,696
# of observations:	61,788	16,374	104,565	33,311
Pseudo R^2	0.080	0.104	0.090	0.093

***Represents significance at the 1 percent level, ** the 5 percent level, * the 10 percent level.

www.ingramcontent.com/pod-product-compliance
Lightning Source LLC
Chambersburg PA
CBHW052024280526
45793CB00005B/1113